BESTSELLER BOOK LAUNCH

A PROVEN 3-STEP SYSTEM FOR LAUNCHING A
BESTSELLER ON AMAZON THAT DEFIES THE
ADVICE OF THE GURUS

RAY BREHM

DAUNTLESS
PROSE

ISBN-13: 978-1-7327830-0-3

READ THIS FIRST!

Enroll in my Bestseller 101 Course FREE!

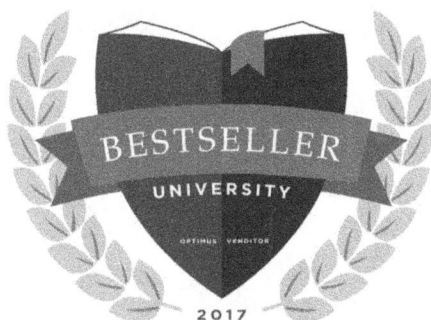

BESTSELLER 101

Just to say thanks for downloading my book, I would like to give you access to my Bestseller 101 Mini-Course FREE!

https://www.bestseller.university/bbl-101

Bestseller 101 utilizes the exact system I use with my Done-For-You clients, to build the first draft of a non-fiction book.

By using a series of questions, and *The Miyagi Approach*, you can spit out a superb first draft, even if you don't know where to start.

Bestseller 101 is a system that helps you focus on your ideal reader so that you can create a compelling manuscript.

Check it out now, free!

https://www.bestseller.university/bbl-101

To all future bestselling authors.....

WHO THIS BOOK IS FOR AND WHO SHOULD NOT READ IT

I hesitate to add this here, but I think the content of this book requires that you know who the intended audience of this book is. This book describes the most efficient way to make your book a bestseller on Amazon.

This book is for you if:

- If you have not published a book yet
- If you have published a book, but did not receive the coveted orange Best Seller banner from Amazon

Best Seller

Those who may not want to read this book

If you have already published a bestselling book, this book

might not be for you. You most likely have your system, and there is always pride involved in a method you have created yourself. In fact, the simplicity and effectiveness of my system I describe may bother you. But then again, if you are open minded, you may gain some new insights into best-seller launches.

One thing I do in this book is let you know about other books of mine, as well as additional training and coaching. I try to keep it subtle, but many people are interested in these services so it helps to reveal them. I also make my living as an author.

So, if seeing links to other things I offer (free and paid) bothers you, you may not want to read any further. This book standalone will give you the results you want, so if you can tolerate me letting you know about other resources, training or services, please read on!

If you have ever written a mean-spirited review of another author (especially anonymously), this book is probably not for you. I am incredibly protective of other authors (and artists) who take the risks to create art by putting it out for the world to see. They are bettering themselves and the world.

I believe in an abundance mindset, and if you do too, I can't wait for you to read this book!

So let's go!!!

INTRODUCTION

THE TALE OF TWO LAUNCHES

WHAT?!?!

I could not believe it!

I was staring at an Amazon Orange Best Seller banner, and I had hardly tried to market the book. The book was *The Author Startup*, and all I had tried to do was write a short eBook on how to write and publish a book quickly. I wasn't concerned with worrying about marketing or bestseller status.

The book was short and to the point (just around 10,000 words). All I was trying to do with that book was prove a point: that you didn't need to worry about marketing or bestseller status to publish a book. You could become a published author without a lot of stress, and gain all of the instant credibility that came with it.

But something else happened as a byproduct.

I stumbled upon an incredible way to streamline a launch

and become a bestseller with minimal effort and maximum effectiveness!

This accidental launch became my **Bestseller Book Launch System.**

I had hit the publish button. I waited a couple of days to clean up my book page, and then I decided just to try a couple of promotions I knew worked (you will see those in the chapter called "The Big Three" later). I set up the two promotions two days apart and made one social media post asking for a launch team on the fly, and 48 hours later I was a Bestseller.

I wondered, "How can that be? Wasn't I supposed to follow all of the gurus' advice and run 100 promotions, set up launch teams, encourage interaction, send emails, post in Facebook groups and all the other things?"

You see 60 days earlier; I had done all that stuff. It worked. But it was a pain in the patoot[1] and caused me all kinds of unnecessary stress. I published *Author Your Success* two months earlier.

Don't get me wrong. The more things you do, the better your chances. But when I dissected that first launch, almost 90% of the work yielded very marginal returns. I decided to do only a few items I knew worked well during my second launch.

Those were:

- Two paid promotions
- 1 Social Media post

Here is the difference:

LAUNCH 1: Author Your Success

- Bestseller
- 1084 free downloads
- Sold around 370 copies in the first month
- Afterwards, sales trickled down to between 0 and one book a day
- I used about 60 Free Promotion Sites
- Paid about $300 across ten paid sites (some of these were paid to promote the book as a free download)

LAUNCH 2: The Author Startup

- Bestseller
- No Free Downloads
- Sold around 200 copies the first week
- Sold around 1000 copies the first month
- 8000 copies been downloaded from Amazon to date (at the time of this writing)
- No Free Promo sites (the book was never free during the launch)
- I used two paid promotions only (around $70)
- Sales stayed high on their own after that first week with no more advertising

What if you are just starting out as an author?

You may be thinking that this may not work for you because you are just starting out. However, I did not have a significant following or an extensive email list of readers. At the time of that second launch, I had an email list of around 40 (three of those were my email addresses). Most of my Facebook friends were old friends from high school.

The system in this book can work for you, so stick with me here!

In this book, I lay out the process so you can follow it easily.

What if your niche is small and unique?

James Archer (the founder of Sharelingo) starting working with me through my **Ghostlauncher** program[2]. He had a book almost ready to launch that supported his big dream of bringing the world closer together by understanding other cultures.

The problem was his book, *Beyond Words*, was that it didn't fit into any typical category or niche. That issue affects not only how the categories are selected, but also how we advertise.

However, we stuck to the exact formula in this book, and within 72 hours he had a bestseller.

What I learned during my second launch, I have used over and over again. It has worked every time for myself and my clients.

I discovered that you only need to follow three simple steps. That, my friend, is what I am about to teach you here so that you can do it too.

But first, I want to tell you why there is no such thing as a free launch.

1 That is the first word that came to mind, and I don't use it that often. The point is, try not to do stuff that is busy work and doesn't give you much return on your time.

2 Ghostlauncher is a program where I handle the entire launch for my clients, see more at Ghostlauncher.com.

1

THERE IS NO SUCH THING AS A FREE LAUNCH

There is no such thing as a FREE LAUNCH. You heard me correctly.

Either the reader pays for your book, or you pay for it.

There is no doubt that you can run a **Free Launch** and end up with a bestseller.[3] But you paid for those free books (by not selling them), and at least some of them could have counted as sales toward your goal of being a bestseller.

What I learned in that second launch is this, a free launch was not needed (even for a newbie).

Here is why I don't like it:

- You spend a lot of time and energy promoting your book for free just to get a little momentum on Amazon before you start charging for your book. When you start charging at least 99 cents, that is the real launch.
- Your rank on Amazon in the "Free" store means nothing toward your goal of being a bestseller.

- For new authors it makes it very confusing, it is like launching twice once free and then once again when paid. Many get confused when they rank well in the free store (not knowing it doesn't help get that orange best seller banner).
- Many people who downloaded free would have paid, especially those who want to help you out. Every sale counts when you are making a bestseller push.

You can give your book away for free, but the time lost promoting it as free is wasted.

Why waste your time?

And there is one more sinister thing at work here.

Many of these free promotions cost money. The others most likely will not work at all (if they get you 5-10 free downloads, that is not working). I have seen authors spending $200-300 just to promote and get people to download their book for free.

I remember during my first launch, I had a spreadsheet going for all the promotions sites I wanted to list on. It had over 100 sites. But each time I went somewhere to submit my promotion, that new site would recommend at least 50 more. Some were duplicates; some were not. In the end, I had this vastly unmanageable spreadsheet that I discovered (after the second launch) had little usefulness in my launch.

I'll admit the free launch approach can and does work. But if you save that $200-300 for advertising your book "on sale" at 99 cents, you can all but guarantee yourself a bestseller.

I will show you how now. Let's talk about the three pillars of a bestseller launch.

3 My understanding is bestseller can be one word or two. I like using one word, but most of the time Amazon uses two. I use both in this book, most likely using two when referring to how Amazon phrases it. I hope that doesn't upset you.

THE THREE STEPS OF A BESTSELLER

What I found during that second launch (*The Author Startup*[4]) was I only needed to focus on three areas, and I could comfortably plan on a bestseller.

The three steps of a bestseller are:

1. Social Proof
2. Niche and Category Selection
3. Sales and Promotions

Ok, that may sound simplistic or even rather obvious, but bear with me. It is simple, straightforward and very efficient.

You won't need hundreds of postings on Facebook, tons of emails to your launch team or email list, and forget about that long list of promo sites.

Each of these pillars requires some attention, but we will walk through them step-by-step.

One last thing, if the book you want to launch as a bestseller is your first book, we will need to do some housekeeping.

Even if you already have published a book, you will want to make sure you understand this next chapter. It is critical to our ultimate goal!

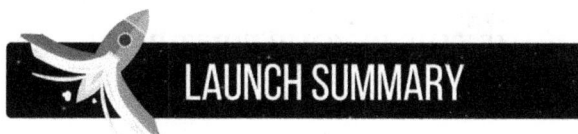
LAUNCH SUMMARY

The three pillars of a bestseller are:

1. Social Proof
2. Niche and Category Selection
3. Sales and Promotions

---

4 If you haven't read *The Author Startup*, you can get a free copy here: theauthorstartup.com.

3

IF THIS IS YOUR FIRST BOOK

The system in this book requires you have a few items in place in regards to your author platform. These are the minimum requirements for a bestseller, so I call the pieces of your "mini" author platform.

Those include:

1. Amazon Author Profile
2. Bookbub Author Profile
3. Book Description on Amazon
4. Editorial Reviews on Amazon

The first two items above cannot be created until you have at least one active published book on Amazon. Therefore, we need to publish our book in preparation of launching.

Publishing vs. Launching

The main point I made in my bestseller *The Author Startup* was this:

Do not try to publish and launch at the same time.

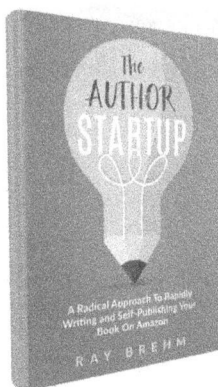

Publishing means you hit the publish button in KDP. Launching is the coordinated effort of marketing towards a bestseller.

Those four items of your "mini" author platform are necessary for your bestseller. Therefore, we need to make sure those are established before we try to launch our book.

We can accomplish this one of two ways. We can publish (in KDP) as either a "**PRE-ORDER**", or "**I AM READY TO RELEASE NOW.**"

Let's discuss those now.

LAUNCH SUMMARY

When you have hit publish, you will want to set these mini platform items up as soon as possible.

1. Amazon Author Profile
   (https://authorcentral.amazon.com/)
2. Bookbub Author Profile
   (https://partners.bookbub.com/users/sign_in)
3. Book Description on Amazon (inside KDP for your book - https://kdp.amazon.com/)
4. Editorial Reviews on Amazon (inside Author Central for you book - https://authorcentral.amazon.com/)

PRE-ORDER VS RELEASE NOW

Let's begin with this suggestion:

**For your very first book use the
"I AM READY TO RELEASE NOW" option.**

Then, until you are ready to publish, you will always "SAVE AS DRAFT."

Page 2 of your book in KDP - Release Now vs. Pre-Order

There are too many things that can become problems if you lock into a Pre-Order date. You can always switch from **Ready to Release Now** to **Pre-Order** later. You cannot go the other direction.

Let's take a look at each option.

I AM READY TO RELEASE NOW

I call this the **Release Now Launch**. For this type of launch, you will first publish your book in KDP. At this point, you aren't letting anyone know the book is available (though it is). Having your book live, but without anyone knowing is what I call **Ninja Mode**

While in **Ninja Mode**, we will set up and clean up the following (from the last chapter):

1. Amazon Author Profile
2. Bookbub Author Profile
3. Book Description on Amazon
4. Editorial Reviews on Amazon

We will also perform Steps 1 (Social Proof) and 2 (Niche and Category Selection) of our Bestseller Book Launch System. I explain those steps in the next two sections of this book.

Then when we are ready to let the world know about our book, we initiate the launch with Step 3 (Sales and Promotions).

The Release Now Launch is by far the best method to use for your first book. The only reason I might be persuaded to suggest using Pre-Order is if you already have a large following.

PRE-ORDER

Jeff Yalden had a large social media following, and he was

very active. His audience was very engaged with him when he posted. He brought me onto his team to handle his entire launch and Ghost launch his book.

Because of his following, I suggested we go the Pre-Order route. The Pre-Order Launch still can utilize Ninja Mode, which we did.

We set up his book for Pre-Order but didn't tell anyone about it (we left it in Ninja Mode).

Pre-Order lets you see your book page live on Amazon and provides the ASIN before the launch. It also allows you to update and submit your categories to KDP (more on the in Step 2).

Ninja Mode time can be used to clean up your book page and description, without worrying about anyone downloading the book yet. People can order, but you still have time to update your manuscript. You can also spread the word about pre-ordering to family and friends if you like.

In Jeff's case, during Pre-Order Ninja Mode we:

- Set up his Amazon Author Central account
- Applied and received his author account on Bookbub (takes 24 hours)
- Applied and received his Bookbub Ads account (takes about a week, but depends on first the author account being approved)
- Set up his book description and Editorial Reviews on his book page
- Picked his niche categories (Step 2) and requested them from KDP

The entire Ninja Mode was about two weeks. Receiving approval for Bookbub Ads is the piece that takes the most time.

At the two week mark, we were still 30 days from his Pre-Order Release Date.

We dropped out of Ninja Mode, ran some Bookbub Ads and he told his following about the book.

Within 48 hours he had the Bestseller Banner for his book *BOOM: One Word to Instantly Inspire Action, Deliver Rewards, and Positively Affect Your Life Every Day!*

It also helped that he got a key endorsement from **Hal Elrod** (*The Miracle Morning*), but he was already on his way to bestseller!

I followed the same process for this book. The result was the same. In fact, I took this concept one step further. See the chapter at the end of this book called "My Ultimate Case Study."

I suggest first trying out the Release Now Launch and saving as a draft until you are ready. The Pre-Order model locks you into a hard date.

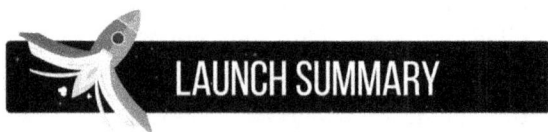

LAUNCH SUMMARY

- Use the **Release Now Launch** your first time out
- Use **Pre-Order Launch** when you have a large following or have already released one book and "know the ropes"

- In either launch, you will have a Ninja Mode period where you get everything tidied up (this is especially critical if it is your first book and you need to set up author pages)
- Read the chapter on "My Ultimate Case Study"

PART I

STEP 1: SOCIAL PROOF

1
_____

YOUR SOCIAL PROOF TEAM

These days, we almost always need some social proof to purchase anything online. Regarding books, we look to the book reviews (after we view the cover and description[5]) to determine if we want to purchase a particular book.

Social proof is what the Yellow Pages used to be.

There is another reason we need the social proof of book reviews. Many promotions require a minimum number of reviews with an average review of four or higher.

Amazon takes reviews and average stars into account when it promotes your book to readers.

So we do need reviews. We need reviews to start, and we want to keep them going indefinitely.

For reviews we focus on in three areas:

- Up front using launch teams
- Requesting reviews inside your book

- Following up with readers who have given you their email for some other special bonus inside your book

Launch Teams

These are people who have agreed to help you launch. They have given up their precious time to read your early drafts and maybe participated with you in some way during the launch. You may have seasoned experts (other authors), other followers or colleagues and editorial reviewers.

They all need to be talked to in different ways depending on their experience level.

I divide them into three groups and send different emails to each:

- Standard launch team - little or no experience but are eager to help. They need the most instruction in your emails.
- Launch Team Pros - Most likely other authors who have participated on other launch teams.
- Executive Launch Team or editorial reviewers - Other established authors who give you reviews in advance for the editorial section of your book page (add these inside author central).

What I have found to be most effective is making it as easy as possible for people to help you. That means very few emails and requests. That is why I like using what I call "Same Day Launch Teams." Let's talk about that now!

LAUNCH SUMMARY

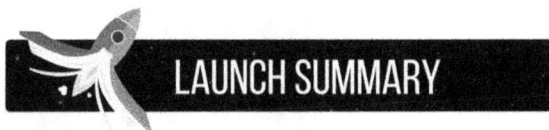

Set up your launch team:

- Standard Launch Team Members
- Launch Team Pros
- Executive Launch Team or editorial reviewers

---

5 For assistance with cover and description, I cover that in *The Author Startup*. Grab a free copy at *theauthorstartup.com.*

2

SAME DAY LAUNCH TEAM

So we mentioned that the best way to get social proof in the form of reviews is to have a launch team. These are people you give insider treatment in the hopes that they will review your book.

The problem is, managing and entertaining the people on your launch teams can require a lot of time and energy. The same goes for your participants.

Most gurus will tell you to form email lists, Facebook groups, and have them apply to join the team and so forth.

After participating in many launch teams myself, I found it incredibly exhausting trying to keep up (from a launch team member perspective).

My thought process is always "How can I make this easier?"

For *The Author Startup*, I came up with an idea. I called it the "SAME DAY LAUNCH TEAM."

Instead of burdening people who are trying to help you launch your book, why not make it as easy as possible.

With a Same Day Launch Team:

- You make the request once the book is out
- Promise only one to two emails
- Request they buy the book for 99¢
- Provide a summary of your book and any buzz words that might be helpful for their use in a review (why not give them some help with the review, so they don't have to think too much)
- I even provided a video summary of the book, for those like me who prefer visual interaction.

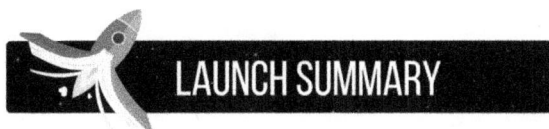

LAUNCH SUMMARY

If you have a large enough network, consider making it easy on them with a Same Day Launch Team.

PART II

STEP 2: NICHE AND CATEGORY SELECTION

3

AMAZON BEST SELLER RANK

ABSR (Amazon Best Sellers Rank) is your key to becoming a bestseller. It also makes your quest measurable.

The Amazon Best Sellers Rank is the way Amazon ranks your book against all others in the Amazon store. You will have a rank in both the free and paid store. You can find the rank midway down the page of any book, under "Product Details."

Product details

File Size: 1206 KB
Print Length: 160 pages
Simultaneous Device Usage: Unlimited
Publication Date: September 10, 2017
Sold by: Amazon Digital Services LLC
Language: English
ASIN: B075JMRTL2
Text-to-Speech: Enabled
X-Ray: Not Enabled
Word Wise: Enabled
Lending: Enabled
Screen Reader: Supported
Enhanced Typesetting: Enabled
Amazon Best Sellers Rank: #5,823 Paid in Kindle Store (See Top 100 Paid in Kindle Store)

ABSR: #5823 in the paid store.

The ABSR in the Paid Store updates in real time based on

sales of your book. That is the number with which you should be concerned.

If you are launching your book as free using KDP select (which I am suggesting you don't bother with), ABSR can be confusing. Though the rank in the Free Store will tell you how well you are doing (how many free downloads of your book you have against all the other free books), it has nothing to do with how well you will do once your book is in the Paid Store (where you get bestseller status). There can be some momentum once you switch, but the truth is it can also give you a false sense of confidence during your launch.

By the way, being a bestseller in the Free Store means nothing as far as bestseller status.

The real number you will be striving for is an ABSR in the Paid Store. If you get your paid ABSR to 12,000 or lower for 48 hours, you can probably be a bestseller. That is if you pick the correct categories for your book. Let's talk about that now.

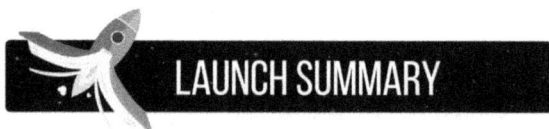
LAUNCH SUMMARY

- Follow your ABSR on your book page
- ABSR in the Paid Store is the one that counts

4

CATEGORY SELECTION

Here are my three rules for category selection:

1. Go to the deepest niche within a category
2. Pick appropriately, but more importantly competitively
3. When in doubt, get help. Becoming a bestseller depends on it.

You can see the top categories a book is in, right below its ABSR #. Those are live links, and you can click on any of those to get to the entire category tree for Kindle books on Amazon.

The key is to pick a category at the very bottom of the tree, which is the least competitive but has at least 100 books. An ABSR of #10,000 or higher fits the bill.

For instance, when I click on Kindle eBooks and then Education & Teaching, I see a list of subcategories. That means I need to go at least one level deeper. I want to niche-down until I can go no deeper.

‹ Any Department
‹ Kindle Store
‹ Kindle eBooks
  Education & Teaching
  Childhood Education
  Higher & Continuing
  Education
  Studying & Workbooks
  Teacher Resources
  Test Preparation

Education & Teaching is not at the bottom of the tree

‹ Any Department
‹ Kindle Store
‹ Kindle eBooks
‹ Education & Teaching
  Studying & Workbooks
  Book Notes
  Study Guides
  Study Skills
  Workbooks

Lowest Categories on the tree - i.e.. Workbooks

If you categorize your book at an intermediate (not lowest) category of the tree, you are now competing against the best books in all of the lower categories.

The difference is subtle but significant. When I checked this, to be #1 in Studying and Workbooks (an intermediate level niche of the category tree), I would have to rank #517 (selling 171 books a day). But if I choose the deepest niche category WORKBOOKS, I only need an ABSR of #15609 (selling 14 books a day).

That is a huge difference. Just how many books each rank sells per day can vary, but an easy way to figure this out is Dave Chesson's Kindle Rank Calculator.

https://kindlepreneur.com/amazon-kdp-sales-rank-calculator/

Alan McComas and I are friends from an author mastermind group. He was launching his book *The Laidback Lifestyle*, and I was just following his launch from afar. I noticed his rank was superb, and his sales were healthy, but he was not a bestseller.

Something was up. I checked the categories Alan was using and saw that he was not niched down to the lowest niches of the category tree. I sent him some suggestions at 2 am, and he implemented them the next morning from the golf course (he lives the laid-back lifestyle).

Within 4 hours he was a bestseller.

In his words, "Ray saved my launch!"

KDP does not make category selection easy

If you look at all the categories on Amazon and find ones that work for your book, that is the first step for categories.

The second step is adding them to your book. The odd thing is, inside KDP where you assign categories to your book, the list does not match what is on Amazon itself.

Here is what you do:

- Inside KDP, always select "Non-classifiable."

Choose up to two categories: x

Choose categories (up to two):

    ☒ Fiction
    ☒ Nonfiction
    ☒ Juvenile Fiction
    ☒ Juvenile Nonfiction
    ☒ Comics & Graphic Novels
    ☒ Education & Reference
    ☒ Literary Collections
    ☑ Non-Classifiable

Selected categories:

Non-Classifiable remove

Cancel   Save

Non-classifiable selection in KDP

Then contact KDP after you have hit the publish button to update your categories. I explain how to do that next!

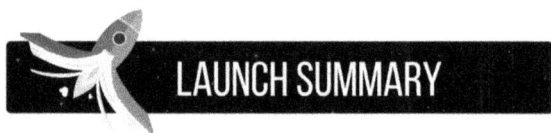

LAUNCH SUMMARY

1. Go to the deepest niche within a category
2. Pick appropriately, but more importantly competitively
3. When in doubt, get help. Becoming a bestseller depends on it. Check out Ghostlauncher.com if you need help.

5

UPDATE KDP WITH NEW CATEGORIES

Once you have your 10 categories, use this process inside KDP to get them updated.

1. Go to Help inside KDP
2. Select the Contact Us Button (bottom left)
3. Select Book Details
4. Click on Categories and Keywords

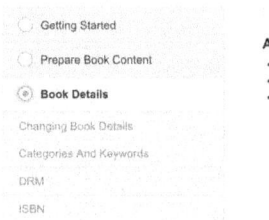

Select Book Details, then Categories and Keywords

A contact box will open on the right.

Or, ask your question here:

Please update my categories

Desired Kindle Store category path(s):

(Example: Kindle Store > Kindle Books > Business & Investing > Reference > Writing)

1. Kindle Store > Kindle eBooks > Education & Teaching > Studying & Workbooks > Workbooks

ℹ Enter as much information as possible.

Send message

Category update with full path of category

- Update the subject line (with something like "Please update my categories").
- Enter your ASIN
- Answer the couple questions about your book (Y or N)
- Provide the 10 new categories (there is space for only 2, just manually create 8 more in the text box starting with "3." You must enter the full path of the category (see example above)
- If you already have categories assigned, or they auto-assigned some (which they might if you picked "Non-classifiable" when you set up the book), make sure you list them in the next section to be removed
- Hit send and they should update them within 24 hours

If you don't remove any existing categories, KDP will send you an email and also not update any. Don't waste time, be sure to remove the old ones!

How do I know when the categories are updated?

KDP will send you an email telling you when they have updated your categories. At this point, they are in the system, but they still might now show up on your Amazon book page (it takes a little time to refresh).

Amazon will only show your top three categories directly under your ABSR #. But if those are the ones you added, you now know your book categories are up to date.

Once you have Social Proof in place, and your Categories selected, it is time to work on sales and promotions.

You can be #1 in a category and not receive the bestseller banner. This is because Amazon's algorithm for determining bestsellers also requires an undisclosed number of sales. So Let's move on to our final step now, sales and promotions!

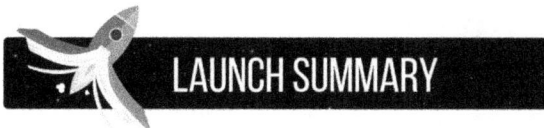

LAUNCH SUMMARY

- Send KDP your updated categories
- Verify they have indeed been updated

PART III

STEP 3: SALES AND PROMOTIONS

6

THE BIG THREE

THE ONLY THREE PROMOTIONS I USE

I am all about simplicity and making things easy. You don't need hundreds of places to promote. If you like posting your book everywhere as a hobby, great! But I don't. I only want to use sources that provide results. For me, in the non-fiction realm, I just use three. The "Big Three."

They are:

- BuckBooks
- BookSends
- Bookbub

You will receive many recommendations, and I am always open to trying new promotions. However, I will only ever try a couple of new things on each launch because I already know what works. I also hate wasting my time!

In a couple of chapters, we will talk about how to schedule these. For now, just make these the foundation of your sales system.

Buckbooks and Booksends will run a promotion to their
lists on a specific day. So scheduling them near each other
and in advance is critical. I have run bestseller launches
merely using these two.

However, a critical mistake many authors make is not
learning about Bookbub. It is the big kahuna here.

When I signed up for Bookbub Ads, I merely hoped I could
match Buckbooks and Booksends in performance. I was
very wrong. The results blew me away!

Let's talk about Bookbub now!

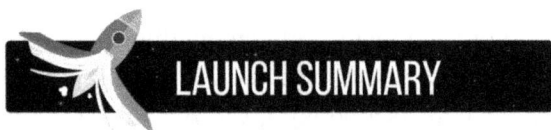

Here is where to go:

- Buckbooks - http://buckbooks.net/promotions/
- Booksends - http://booksends.com/advertise.php
- Bookbub - See next chapter.

7

BOOKBUB

THE GRANDADDY OF THEM ALL

"**There must be some mistake,**" I thought. A glitch in KDP or something. The Author Startup had been a Bestseller for 30 days and was consistently selling around 30 books a day.

But on this day, when I logged into KDP there was a spike in my sales. I had sold well over 100, and it was only 7 am.

Of course, I was pumped. But I wanted to understand why. I was about to go on a "no-phones" and "no-outside world" retreat, that night, but I had to know why this had happened. It was crazy good!

I suddenly remembered I had been accepted into Bookbub Ads and had run a test advertisement just for kicks the day before this retreat. I logged into Bookbub, looked at my ad, and sure enough, I had 100s of clicks on my ad that apparently resulted in sales.

I had stumbled onto Bookbub Ads just poking around on their site. But I had found something incredible.

"I tried Bookbub, and they didn't accept my Ad."

That is the most common response I receive when I ask if someone has set up Bookbub Ads for their book.

Bookbub is the unspoken secret weapon for many authors.

Bookbub's tagline is "Reach millions of power readers." As of right now, it is the most potent advertising source you can use.

It is also the most confusing for new users because they provide two different methods of advertising. Let's look at them.

FEATURED DEALS (not what we will use)

Bookbub is well known for its **Featured Deals**. You have to apply for Featured Deals, and be prepared to prepay (somewhere around $500) for a selected genre. Bookbub looks at your book, the genre and some other criteria (page count must be over 100 for example). Then they determine if they will accept your ad. Most ads do not get approved.

Not to worry, once you have established yourself as an author, your Featured Deals applications may be more readily accepted. But why bother with Featured Deals, when there is a lower cost of entry that provides more control with their **Bookbub Ads** feature?

BOOKBUB ADS (use this!!!)

Bookbub Ads is a Pay-Per-Impression system built right into your Bookbub Author login. You do have to apply for it currently, and it takes about two weeks for approval.

I have set up countless clients (and myself) on Bookbub Ads, and never has anyone not been approved. Getting approval means that you are free to now run as many ads as you want to the millions of Bookbub power readers.

Bookbub provides real-time statistics on your Ads including impressions and click-through-rate. If that all sounds confusing, it isn't. Bookbub makes it easy.

Impressions are how many readers see your advertisement (via an email Bookbub sends out to readers).

A reader signs up to a specific genre, and even specific authors, to receive emails on "deals" for those types of books. Those reader interests provide an excellent opportunity to target a particular reader.

For instance, if I want to target a reader who reads business books and also likes Tony Robbins, it is straightforward to do. That fact alone makes the tool more powerful than Amazon's own Amazon Marketing Services (AMS).

My experience has been that it costs around $10 per 1000 impressions. That means, for $10, 1000 people will see my ad. If I receive a 1% CTR (Click-Through-Rate), ten people have clicked on my ad. For my books, that means around eight people will buy.

You can then use your Bookbub stats page to determine how many clicks you had that day, and your KDP stat page to see how many purchases. Now there is always a chance people are finding your book from another source, so I then subtract the average amount of sales from the days before the Bookbub Ad from the sales the day of the Bookbub ad, and that will give me a pretty good idea how my ad is doing.

Here is an example:

From Bookbub

- 10,000 Impressions ($100)
- 1% CTR (or 100 clicks)

From KDP Reports

- Average sales before Ad: 10 per day
- Average sales during the Ad: 122 per day

If this was a real example, for $100 I probably would receive 112 sales. At 99 cents I may lose a little money, but my ABSR is sure to be stellar.

I also run multiple ads and compare the CTR from the Bookbub stats to see which ads are performing best.

I like this approach because you can spend a lot less per click and per sale using Bookbub Ads, than you can with some of these other $40 promotion sources.

When I helped Carrie Sechel launch her Bestseller BASE Jump: Finding Yourself In An Unfulfilling Professional World, we started with Bookbub and never needed to use the other two promotions from "The Big Three."

She gave me a list of authors who speak to her target market, like Tony Robbins, Brendon Burchard, and Sheryl Sandberg. We targeted those people with one ad, and her incredible book became a bestseller. You can do it too!

The Big Three, and especially Bookbub will bring you the sales. You just need to schedule them correctly for maximum impact on your launch. Let's talk about how to plan The Big Three them next!

- Make sure to apply for your Author Profile on Bookbub first. That takes 24 - 48 hours. Then you can apply for Bookbub Ads.
- You can read more about Bookbub Ads here. https://insights.bookbub.com/what-are-bookbub-ads/
- You can read more about FEATURED DEALS here. https://insights.bookbub.com/bookbub-featured-deals-vs-bookbub-ads-whats-the-difference/

LAUNCH AND PROMOTION SCHEDULE

I only launch on three days of the week, Tuesday, Thursday or Sunday. In fact, always on a Tuesday. It is common industry practice to launch on those three days. Tuesday has been proven to yield the best results.

Don't ever try to do anything on Friday; your readers most likely have "weekend fever"!

There are two things we want to do with our Bestseller Book Launch:

1. Concentrate sales to get bestseller status
2. Stay at #1 in a category for at least three days

To do that we want to line up our "Big Three" promotions, and any social media were posting to occur right on and after launch day.

Let's look at some definitions:

- **Publish Day** - the day we push publish in KDP

- **Launch Day** - the day we tell everyone the book is there
- **Release Day** - For the Release Now Launch, the Release Day is the same as the Publish Day. For the Pre-Order Launch, the Release Day is the Pre-Order date.
- **Ninja Mode** - the time period between Publish Day and Launch Day

We want to run our "Big Three" from Launch Day forward.

Here are a couple of sample schedules for both the Release Now Launch and the Pre-Order Launch.

Release Now Launch - Sample Schedule

Release Now allows you to move these dates if you run into any problems.

- Day 1 - **Publish Day / Release Day**
- Day 1-14 - Ninja Mode (Steps 1 and 2)
- Day 14 - **Launch Day** (most likely a Tuesday)
- Day 14 - Buckbooks (schedule this in advance)
- Day 14 and ongoing - Bookbub
- Day 16 - Booksends (schedule this in advance)

Pre-Order Launch - Sample Schedule 1
Ninja Mode Only

Pre-Order is strict on the dates, but allows you to create a buzz and gather sales before anyone even views your book. There are two approaches to this type of launch. You can mimic the Release Now Launch and just use the

Pre-Order period entirely as Ninja Mode to clean up things.

- Day 1 - **Publish Day**
- Days 1-29 - Ninja Mode you will do Steps 1 and 2
- Day 30 - **Release Day / Launch Day** (most likely a Tuesday)
- Day 30 - Buckbooks (schedule this in advance)
- Day 30 and ongoing - Bookbub
- Day 32 - Booksends (schedule this in advance)

Pre-Order Launch - Sample Schedule 2
Pre-Order Bestseller

If you want to launch and go for bestseller during the Pre-Order period, you can use this schedule. I now use this type of launch almost exclusively.

The difference here is you will be in Ninja Mode for the first part of your Pre-Order period; you will launch while you are still in Pre-Order. Here you will notice that Publish Day, Launch Day and Release Day are all different dates.

- Day 1 - **Publish Day**
- Days 1-13 - Ninja Mode you will do Steps 1 and 2
- Day 14 - **Launch Day** (most likely a Tuesday)
- Day 14 and ongoing - Bookbub (and social media)
- Day 30 - **Release Day** (most likely a Tuesday)
- Day 30 - Buckbooks (schedule this in advance)
- Day 32 - Booksends (schedule this in advance)

For this last one, the Release Day being on a Tuesday is less critical because you have already launched. In fact, a Sunday may be more preferable.

The number of days in between each date aren't critical until you are lining up the Buckbooks and Booksends ads. Those only run one day each, so we want to make sure we batch them close to each other.

The order of these samples is probably the best order to test the launches. Start with the Release Now Launch. Then try the Pre-Order Ninja Mode Only and finally the Pre-Order Bestseller.

Now that you have a plan, there is one other critical element that you need to do. You need to keep track of what happens during your launch so you can improve the next one. Let's talk about that next!

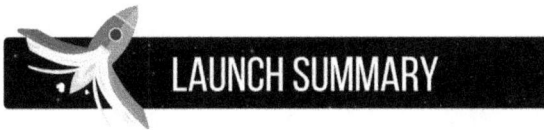

LAUNCH SUMMARY

- Launch on Tuesdays
- Use the Release Now Launch first to "learn the ropes"
- Use the Pre-Order Ninja Mode Only Launch to get experience with Pre-Order
- Use the Pre-Order Bestseller ongoing to crank out your multiple bestsellers!

PART IV

THE LAUNCH AND BEYOND

9

JOURNAL YOUR LAUNCH

A lot of the chaos around the launch is you can quickly lose track of what promos are running, and when. Also, what you should be doing each day of the launch, in addition to simply clicking your sales page in KDP to see how you are doing, or your books age on Amazon to see your rank.

Actually, if you organize it properly, you can do that without stressing about all the things you should be doing.

One of the best things I did during my launch was keep a list of all the things I would do better next time. It was written on the back of a utility bill envelope, but at least I was writing it down.

Organizing a launch and making it better each time means keeping track of what went well and what didn't. Write it down!

LAUNCH SUMMARY

I am working on a *Bestseller Book Launch Journal* to go with this book. I expect to release it in 2018. Stay tuned.

10

NEED MORE TO DO?

OTHER THINGS YOU CAN DO IF YOU HAVE TIME

Here are some ideas for other things you can do to help your book:

- **Release another book** - having two books out each raises the profile of the other
- **Make your book shorter** (10-15,000 words are in, 100,000 are out)
- **DO NOT do the cover yourself** - covers sell, hire a pro
- Use **AMS (Amazon Marketing Services)** to market your book directly on Amazon - I normally add this after I launch

A couple of weeks after I released The Author Startup, I published one of my free books Track Your Success just for kicks.

Interestingly, both books started immediately showing up in more places on Amazon. This "piggybacking" can be very useful to your book.

LAUNCH SUMMARY

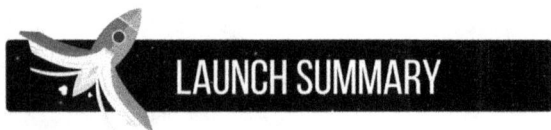

Free training on how to use AMS check out Dave Chessun's Free course at Kindlepreneuer.com

DEAD SEA TROLLS

WHY BAD REVIEWS ARE GOOD FOR YOUR BOOK

"In many ways, the work of a critic is easy. We risk very little, yet enjoy a position over those who offer up their work and their selves to our judgment. We thrive on negative criticism, which is fun to write and to read. But the bitter truth we critics must face, is that in the grand scheme of things, the average piece of junk is probably more meaningful than our criticism designating it so."

— ANTON EGO - THE CRITIC IN RATATOILLE

When you launch your bestseller or any book for that matter, you will get some bad reviews. It is not a matter of if, but when.

I want to put bad reviews into context for you.[12]

You have spent a lot of time creating your work, and bad reviews hurt. That is our emotional side, and as creators, we almost all have a lot of emotion.

The first thing I want to do is distinguish between two types of bad reviews. The first is a bad review that has some merit. Maybe you have some typos, or hey, it is your first book, it isn't going to be perfect! That is ok, use the review as constructive feedback, improve your writing and move on.

DEAD SEA TROLLS

The second type of bad reviews is merely those written by trolls. Or should I say there is one troll for all of Amazon? That troll's name is "Amazon Customer." They try to say something witty like "Save your 99 cents" or "Don't buy this book" or "Wish I hadn't wasted my time."

Ignore them, or mentally say to yourself, "I wish I hadn't wasted my time reading this troll drivel."

There are just some people in life who don't want to make an effort to become an expert in something. They believe they can take a short cut to stardom, and criticize, and that makes them an expert. Let them dream!

8 Laws of why BAD reviews
are GOOD for your book

Now, that that's over, let's set all emotion aside and take a look at bad reviews from a logical standpoint. They are good for your book in many ways.

Here are my 8 Laws of why BAD reviews are GOOD for your book:

1. **Bad reviews can help you fix things.** As I said, if

the review points out some deficiencies in your work, they have helped you improve your book. So we fix it and move on.

2. **There is no such thing as bad press.** Have you ever heard the phrase "there is no such thing as bad press." Right? There are so many times something bad happens to a company or someone, but it brings them so much extra attention and advertising, that they come out ahead in the end. The bad review is like an advertisement. And many times what someone finds offensive and writes the bad review about is a positive for the next person who reads the review. Let that sink in for a moment. The most straightforward example is politics. If a reviewer from political B reads a book favoring political party A, they leave a bad review (almost guaranteed, sometimes after only reading the title). But when a reader that favors political party A reads that review, he or she is now even more likely to read the book. If you make a stand, pick a side, and go deeper, your book is better. And you will get bad reviews.

3. **Troll-like reviews are actually very helpful.** If the reviews are ridiculous, people ignore them (yet they add legitimacy to your book). If your book has all five-star reviews, that will seem fishy to the prospective reader. In fact, when you launch, you have favorable readers writing your early reviews. You will sometimes get a bad review just for that (I know I have). So if I am looking at a book, if I see all 5-star reviews, I think it is fishy. If I notice mostly five stars, and a couple one stars, I go and read the

1-star reviews. When I realize they are troll-like reviews, or even non-troll pointing out some general things, I say ok. These bad reviews don't mean anything to me. But now I will read the book because it wasn't all five stars and the one stars were not meaningful to me.

4. **You are not a real author until you get a bad review.** The plain fact of the matter is that every real author, every book out there has people who didn't like it. Once your book starts becoming big enough that a broader audience is consuming it, you will get negative reviews. So, congrats, you just hit the big time.

5. **If your book pleases everyone, then you are not being passionate enough** or going deep enough into your topic. As I said before, pick a side, make a stand and go deeper. Your book is not worth reading unless you take a side on your issue, and that will make somebody mad. So, if you get nothing else, remember this, your book is not worth reading unless you piss some people off.

6. **Reviews become a numbers game after 50 or so.** What does that mean? Every review adds to your count, and once you get above 50, you are focused on getting 100 reviews. Every subsequent review, regardless of how many stars they gave, increases that number. Think of it this way, would you rather have 50 reviews for an average of 5 stars or 100 reviews with an average of 4.8? I know I want the 100. So once I get over 50, and I get a negative review I stand up, and say out loud imagining the person who wrote the bad review in front of me,

"Thank you. You are helping me, and you don't even know it!"

7. **People who leave Anonymous reviews are not authorities; they are trolls.** People are wising up to this. But you cannot guide your life by feedback from people who criticize anonymously. You cannot shape your book, your course, or how you feel about yourself by people who don't even dare to sign their name to a critique. So ignore them. They look foolish not you.

8. **Great leaders are not easily offended.** This is what separates you from the troll. By writing a book, you have become a leader. Michael Hyatt said in a blog post, "Being offended is a choice. You get to decide how you react to it."

If you have read much about *The Hero's Journey*, as described by Joseph Campbell, you understand that you are the hero in this story.

You the author of the book, are the hero. You are trying to help or entertain people. The trolls are the villains, the people trying to bring the hero down. It is up to you to take the high road and forge ahead like a hero.

And here is the thing, what makes the hero, in any story or life, a great hero? The villains.

Embrace the bad review, and move forward. You are now a real author. You are a hero.

LAUNCH SUMMARY

"If you write (or paint or dance or sculpt or sing, I suppose), someone will try to make you feel lousy about it, that's all." — **Stephen King, On Writing: A Memoir of the Craft**

12 Actually, this chapter is useful for any endeavor you partake in where you can get bad feedback. To give you another great quote, here is the critic from Ratatouille

MY ULTIMATE CASE STUDY

A SECRET FROM THE LAUNCH OF BESTSELLER BOOK LAUNCH

With this book, the Bestseller Book Launch I did something a little crazy to illustrate how robust this system is.

This book became a bestseller on September 19, 2017, while it was in Pre-Order (Release Date was October 22, 2017).

At that time, I hadn't even completed the first draft.

There is a reason I did that for this book.

I wanted to show you that with a proper launch (Pre-Order Bestseller Launch), one can sell enough books to become a bestseller, even before the final draft of the book is complete.

The Bestseller Book Launch System works and is very powerful!

That being said, here are a few caveats:

- I am an expert in all the content in this book, so I was confident the book would be outstanding
- I had already taught a course (Bestseller University)

about all the concepts in this book, so the script for that course was the rough draft for this book

- The book has to have outstanding content, or it will be dead in the water and even receiving the banner will not save it. I had the material and proof of concept already complete, just not the draft for the book.

- Do not try this at home. I only did this to illustrate how potent this Bestseller Book Launch System is and I probably will never do it again. If a book is released from Pre-Order before the finished content uploads to Amazon, it would be catastrophic to author's reputation and Amazon account.

- Many companies and artists offer their products or services for sale before completion. They accomplish these things through pre-orders or Kickstarter type campaigns. It is not unusual, but I would not recommend it for you or your book.

The content has to be amazing. But so does the marketing, and that is what the Bestseller Book Launch System does.

There is a reason they call it "Best SELLING Author" not "Best WRITING Author."

Thanks for reading and I look forward to your book being a bestseller!

ABOUT THE AUTHOR

Ray Brehm is a Best-Selling Author, Entrepreneur, and founder of Dauntless Prose. Dauntless Prose helps entrepreneurs who are short on time, write and publish their books. Ray also provides guidance through online courses at his website raybrehm.com.

With a background in Real Estate and Information Technology, Ray has become an emerging writer focusing on enabling Entrepreneurs to become authors.

Ray is a member of the **National Academy of Best-Selling Authors™** and **The National Association of Experts, Writers & Speakers®**. Ray was also recently interviewed on **America's Top Authors™**, which aired on **CNN, CNBC** and **FOX News** in the spring of 2017.

To reach Ray:
www.raybrehm.com

WHAT DO I DO NEXT?

Getting started is often the biggest hurdle. If you are like me, you may have read this book before you even started writing your draft.

I offer some programs to get people moving quickly towards their goals.

Haven't started your draft yet?

If you haven't started your draft, that should be your primary focus until completed. Need some help? Check out my free Bestseller 101 course. It teaches you how to build a draft quickly using my Ultimate Authority Book Template. This template is what I use with my Done-For-You clients. I ask them questions directly from the template, and their answers create the draft. (See more about Bestseller 101 in the next chapter)

Need help with a launch?

Get a coach or consultant to help you. Sometimes it just makes sense to have a team help you with your launch. I offer this to select clients via my Ghostlauncher Program.

No time to write a book?

I take on 3 or 4 clients a year, and via a series of interviews write their books for them. I call it my Done-For-You program. You can also search on Google for these types of services as well.

Want to jump right to Bestseller Status?

One of my most sought-after programs is called The Co-Author Project. You write one chapter, I handle the rest and guarantee you become a bestselling author. You guessed it; I use the system in this book! It is called The Co-Author Project. You can read more about it after the next chapter.

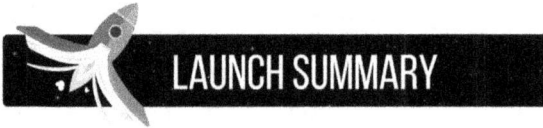

LAUNCH SUMMARY

1. **Bestseller 101** (read more in the next chapter)
2. **Ghostlauncher** Program
3. **Done-For-You** (contact me)
4. **The Co-Author Project** (chapter after next)

BESTSELLER 101

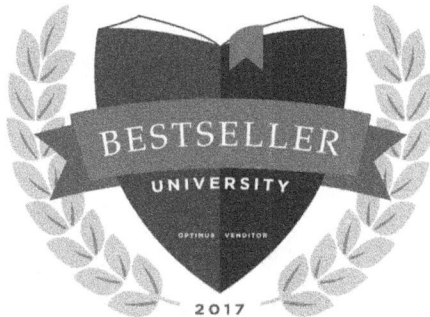

BESTSELLER 101

Bestseller 101 utilizes the exact system I use with my Done-For-You clients, to build the first draft of a non-fiction book. I call it The Ultimate Authority Book Template. This has not even been published yet, but I offer training on it in my Bestseller 101 course.

By using a series of questions, and *The Miyagi Approach*, you can spit out a superb first draft, even if you don't know where to start.

Bestseller 101 is a system that helps you focus on your ideal reader so that you can create a compelling manuscript.

Enrollment is free! Get your draft done!

https://www.bestseller.university/bbl-101

FASTRACK A BESTSELLER!

There is no question getting that first book done and published is by far the hardest thing to do. When you add launching it as a Bestseller to the list, it can add up.

I started the Co-Author Project for authors who want to get their name on a bestselling book as soon as possible. It launches their author platform and forever gives them the right to call themselves **BESTSELLING AUTHORS.**

If all you had to worry about was one chapter, and everything else was taken care of, would that help?

A few times a year, I gather a group of authors and we co-author a book. I make sure, in fact, **I guarantee** to the other authors, that **it will be a Bestseller.**

I call it The Co-Author Project, and you can read about it and sign up for consideration here:

https://www.co-author.me

If you are interested, make sure to get on that Co-Author list, because those are the people who hear about it first and get first chance to join me on my next Bestselling book! The spots fill up every time we open it up!

https://www.co-author.me

REVIEW REQUEST

Most of us don't spend the time to review items we like. We only write reviews when we are dissatisfied. In reality, the best way to get more good products out there is to let people know that you are happy with them.

What you might not know is how valuable even a one-sentence review is to an author. It is like gold. Most authors read every review. I would go as far as to say that reviews are more valuable than sales early on for each book.

If this book helped you, and I hope it has, would you please leave me an honest review on Amazon?

Reviews: Bestseller Book Launch on Amazon

http://amzn.to/2zfX3lB

www.ingramcontent.com/pod-product-compliance
Lightning Source LLC
Chambersburg PA
CBHW071504070426
42452CB00041B/2294